The NYSTROM Block Buddy ATLAS

NYSTROM

DIVISION OF HERFF JONES, INC.

Executive Editors	Charles Novosad
	Tina Tinkham Garrison
Project Manager	Joan Pederson
Cartographic Manager	Christine D. Bosacki
Character Illustrations	Chris Sharp
Neighborhood Illustrations	Skip Baker
	Trey Yancy
Nystrom Computer Cartography	Charlaine Wilkerson
	Phyllis Kawano
	Bonnie Jones
Photographic Research	Charlotte Goldman
	Susana Darwin
Book Design	The Quarasan Group, Inc.
Educational Consultant	Dr. JoAnne Buggey

For information about ordering this atlas and other components of the Exploring Where & Why program, call toll-free 800-621-8086.

1999 Edition
Copyright © 1998 NYSTROM Division of Herff Jones, Inc.
3333 Elston Avenue, Chicago, Illinois 60618

10 9 8 7 6 5 4 3 2   01 00 99 98

ISBN: 0-7825-0657-7   Product Code Number: 9A97A
Printed in U.S.A.

Contents

This list tells what lies ahead!

What do neighborhoods

Winding streets

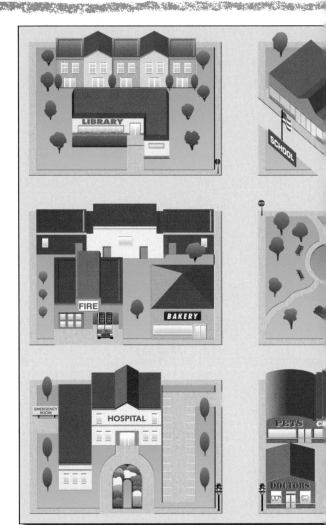

This neighborhood has streets and places to live and work. So does yours.

Houses close together

How are these neighborhoods alike?

look like?

Tall buildings

How tall are the buildings near YOU?

Straight streets

How are they different?

Are any of these like YOUR neighborhood?

Houses far apart

Where do people live?

🌲 Row houses

🌲 Mobile homes

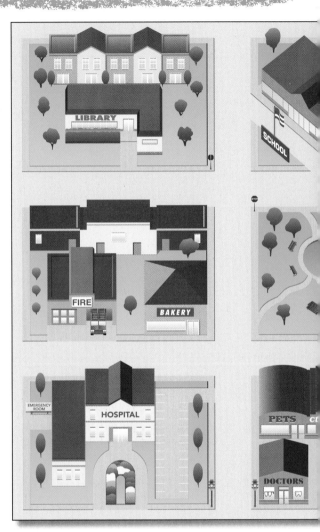

Some people in this neighborhood live in apartments. Others live in houses.

🌲 Big house

Find the places where people live.

🌲 Apartment building

Which home is most like yours?

Farm house

Ranch house

Small house

High-rise apartments

Where do people work?

Shoe store

Find the places where people work.

This neighborhood has places to live. It also has places to work and shop.

Mail route

Restaurant

🌲 Grocery store

Where do people work in YOUR neighborhood?

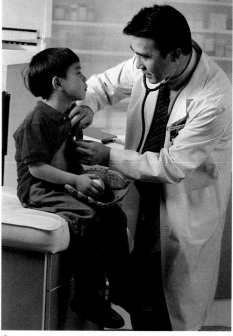

🌲 Doctor's office

🌲 Pet store

What are our needs and

🌲 Fun with friends

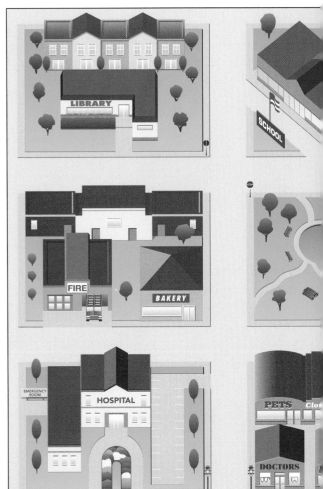

Which things are wants?

This neighborhood has things people need. It also has things they want.

🌲 Food

🌲 Clothing

wants?

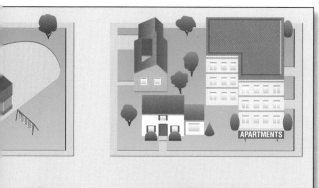

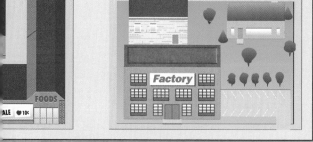

Which things are needs?

🌿 Transportation

🌿 Communication

🌿 Place to live

Which are both wants AND needs?

Where do you like to go?

🦶 **Playground**

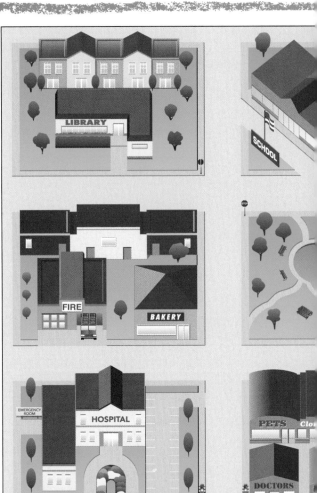

This neighborhood has places to enjoy. Almost every neighborhood has places like them.

How many places like these can you find here?

🦶 **Library**

🦶 **Soccer field**

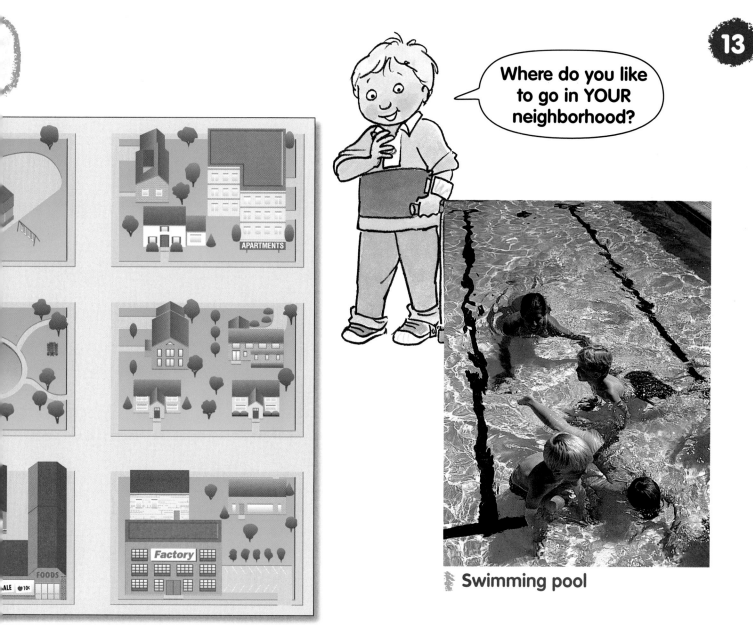

Where do you like to go in YOUR neighborhood?

🌲 Swimming pool

🌲 School

🌲 Museum

How do neighborhoods

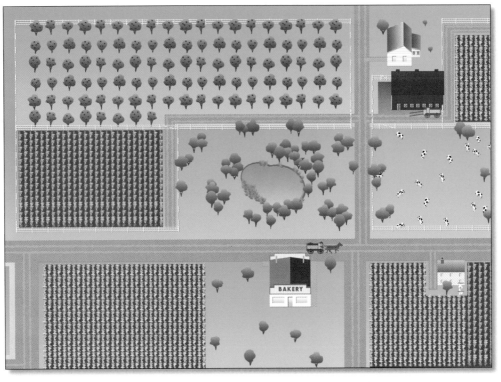

1 Few people lived here at first. All the streets and homes were new.

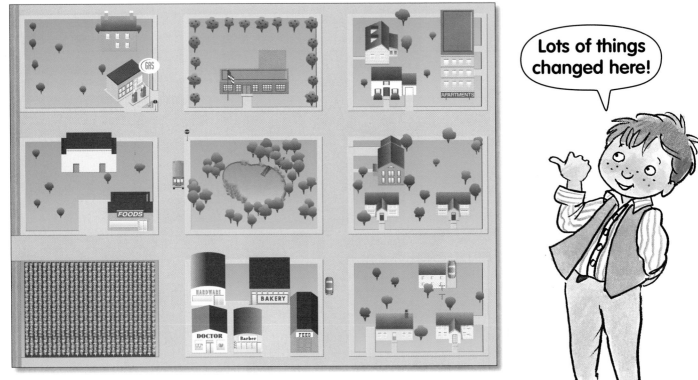

2 More and more people came. They built new places to live and work.

Lots of things changed here!

change?

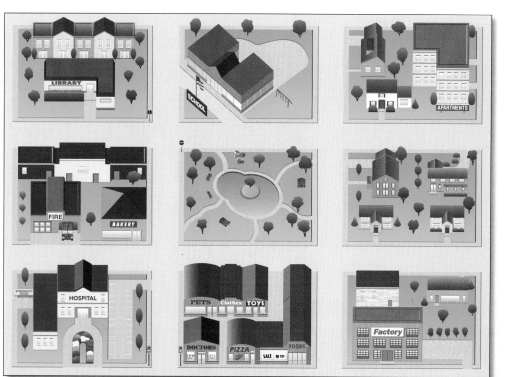

3 Over the years the neighborhood kept changing. Today it looks like this.

4 This is how the neighborhood might look in the future.

What is a model?

🌲 Model of a neighborhood

Find this neighborhood on pages 12 and 13.

Most models are smaller than the real thing.

🌲 Dinosaur model

Playhouse

Many playthings are simple models.

Some models look very real.

Toy car

What is a globe?

The earth from far out in space

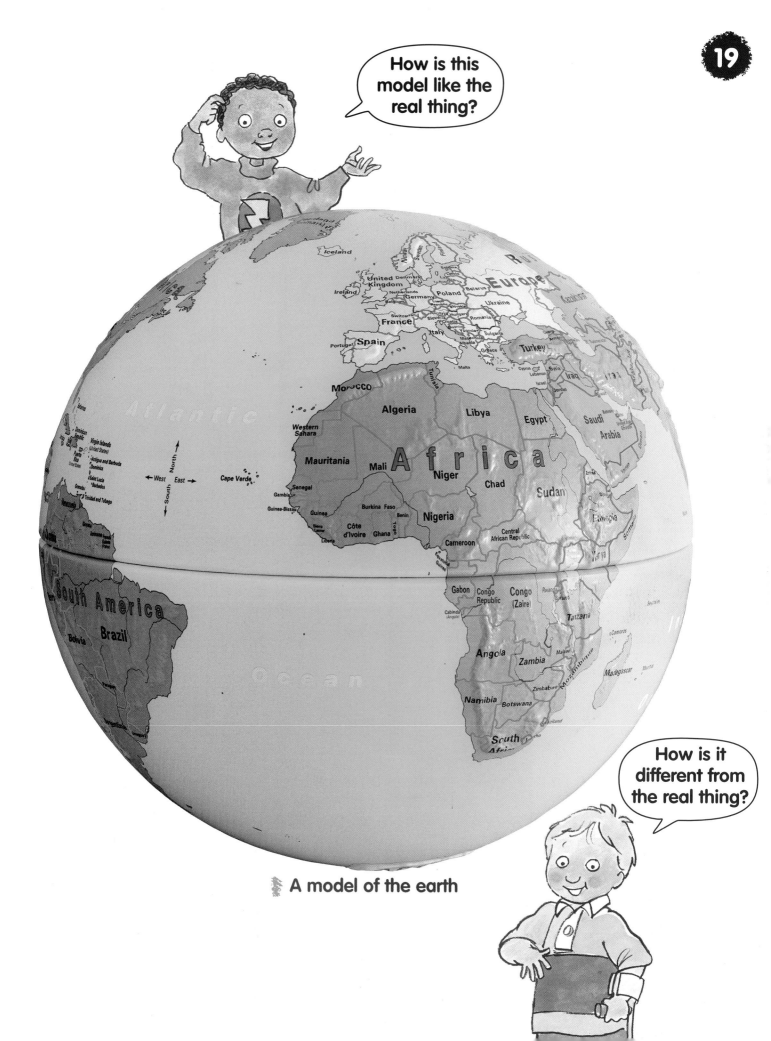

A model of the earth

What is a map?

We found this building in a park.

1 **View from the ground** What we see when we're walking

The same park is shown in all the pictures.

2 **Bird's-eye view** Seen by a bird in flight

3 **View from an airplane**   Looking straight down

How is the map LIKE the view above?

How is the map DIFFERENT from the view above?

4 **Map view**   A special drawing looking straight down

How do maps show

Pacific Ocean

California

🌲 **Coastline** Black line between land and water colors

Elk River

🌲 **River** Wavy black line

What is usually blue on maps?

Pine Lake

🌲 **Lake** Blue area with land all around it

places?

Find these six terms in the glossary.

Mountain Gray shadows

Cascade Mountains

Country capital Red star in a red circle

Maryland

Washington, D.C.

Virginia

Boundary Red line

Welcome to UTAH

Utah

Arizona

How do maps show your

On this photo from outer space,
your country is outlined.

country?

Name your country and its continent.

North
America

United
States

Atlantic
Ocean

Pacific

Equator

Ocean

South
America

🖌 Here continents are different colors.
Red lines show country boundaries.

We made the ocean light blue on both maps.

Russia

Arctic
Ocean

Alaska
(United States)

Canada

Pacific

Ocean

Hawaii
(United States)

United States

Atlantic
Ocean

Gulf of
Mexico

Mexico

Cuba

OCEAN
BLUE

🖌 Here color makes your country stand out.
Red lines show state boundaries.

Where is your state?

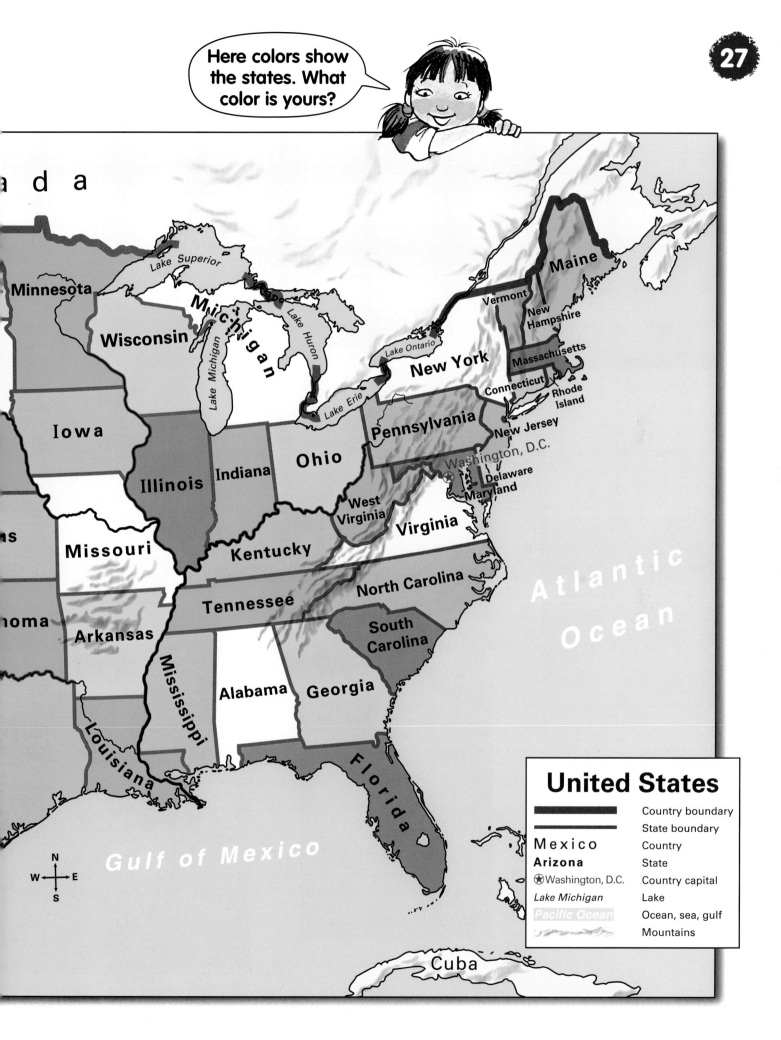

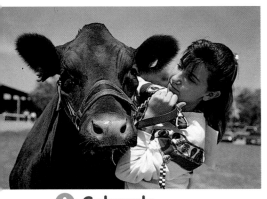

Ⓐ Colorado

Ⓑ Washington

Ⓒ California

AK

Ⓑ WA

OR · ID

NV

HI

Ⓒ CA

AZ

Ⓓ

Where might you meet kids like you?

Ⓓ Arizona

Ⓔ Minnesota

like you?

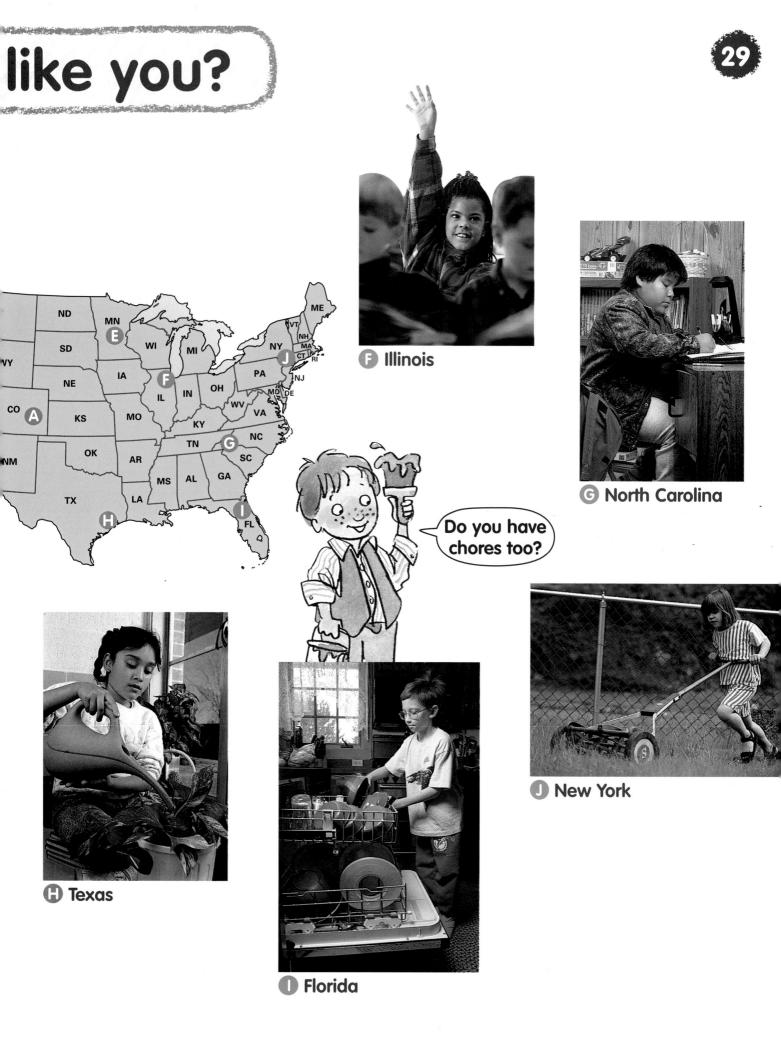

F Illinois

G North Carolina

Do you have chores too?

H Texas

I Florida

J New York

How can you see the

A globe can't show the whole world at once.

You see something new each time you turn a globe.

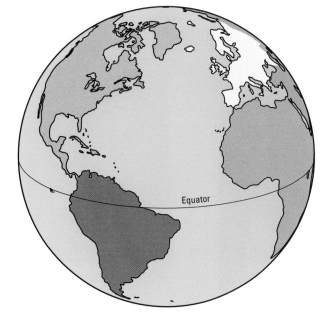

whole world at once?

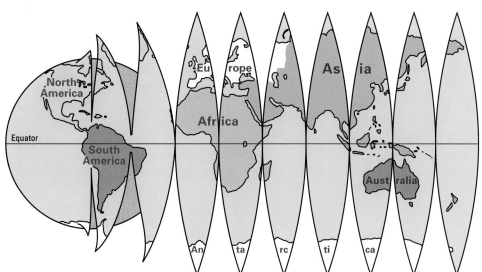

When you peel something round, its skin tears.

🐛 Only a peeled globe can show the whole world at once.

Which is easier to read?

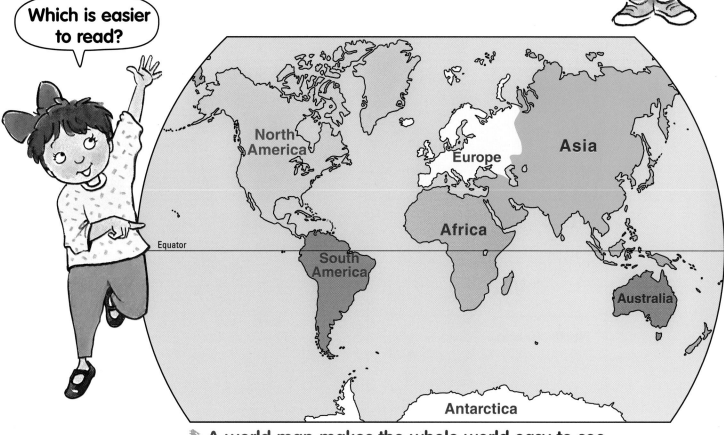

🐛 A world map makes the whole world easy to see.

Where are the

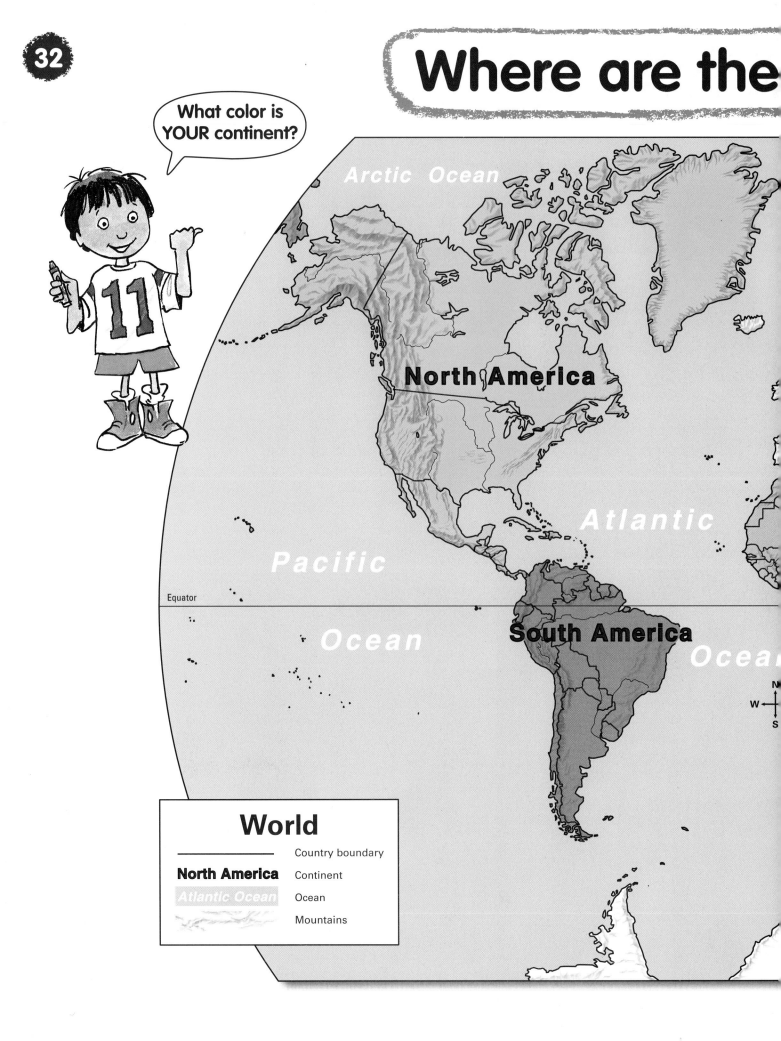

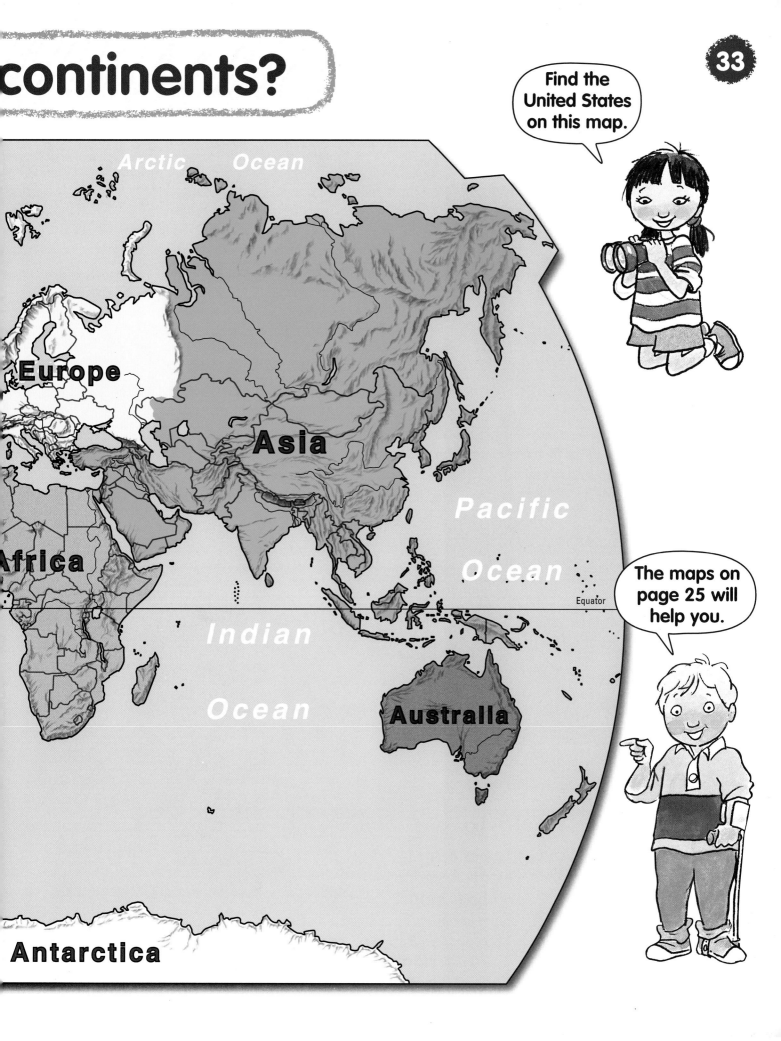

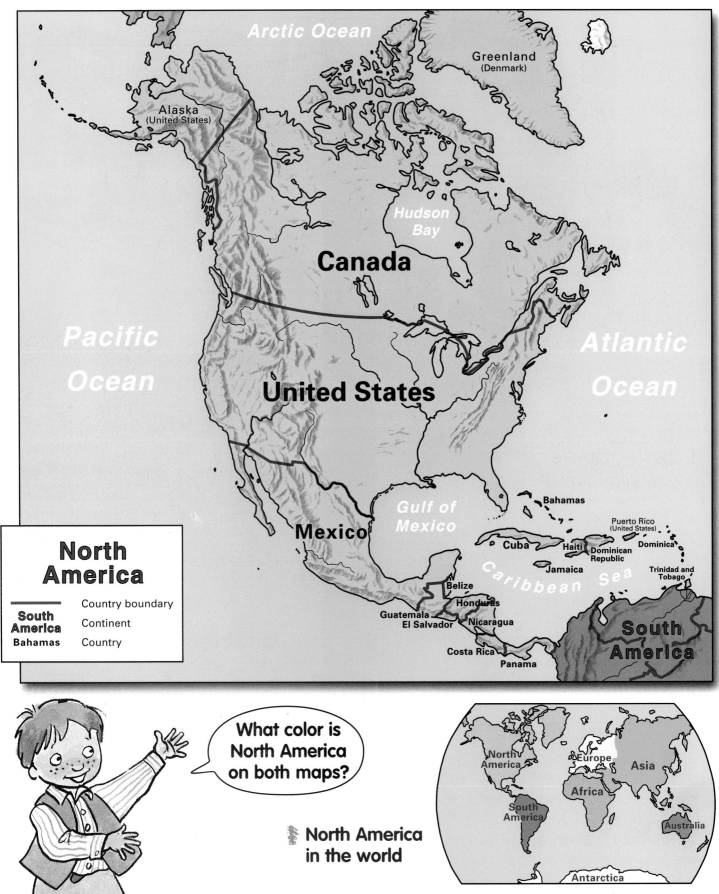

North America

——	Country boundary
South America	Continent
Bahamas	Country

Map labels: Arctic Ocean, Greenland (Denmark), Alaska (United States), Hudson Bay, Canada, Pacific Ocean, United States, Atlantic Ocean, Mexico, Gulf of Mexico, Bahamas, Puerto Rico (United States), Cuba, Haiti, Dominican Republic, Dominica, Jamaica, Caribbean Sea, Trinidad and Tobago, Belize, Honduras, Guatemala, El Salvador, Nicaragua, Costa Rica, Panama, South America

What color is North America on both maps?

North America in the world

World map labels: North America, Europe, Asia, Africa, South America, Australia, Antarctica

North America like you?

Boy in Guatemala

Skiers in Canada

Family in Mexico

What color are country names on this map?

School children in Mexico

Boy in Puerto Rico

How are children in South

North
America

Venezuela

Guyana

Colombia

Suriname

French Guiana
(France)

Atlantic

Ocean

Equator

Ecuador

Equator

Peru

Brazil

Pacific

Ocean

Bolivia

Paraguay

Chile

Uruguay

Atlantic

Ocean

Argentina

South America

————	Country boundary
North America	Continent
Paraguay	Country

Name the continent
that touches
South America.

South America
in the world

North
America

Europe

Asia

Africa

South
America

Australia

Antarctica

America like you?

Students in Venezuela

Basketball players in Argentina

Do you ever shop with YOUR mother?

Boy in Bolivia

Mother and son in Brazil

Boy and alpaca in Peru

How are children in Africa

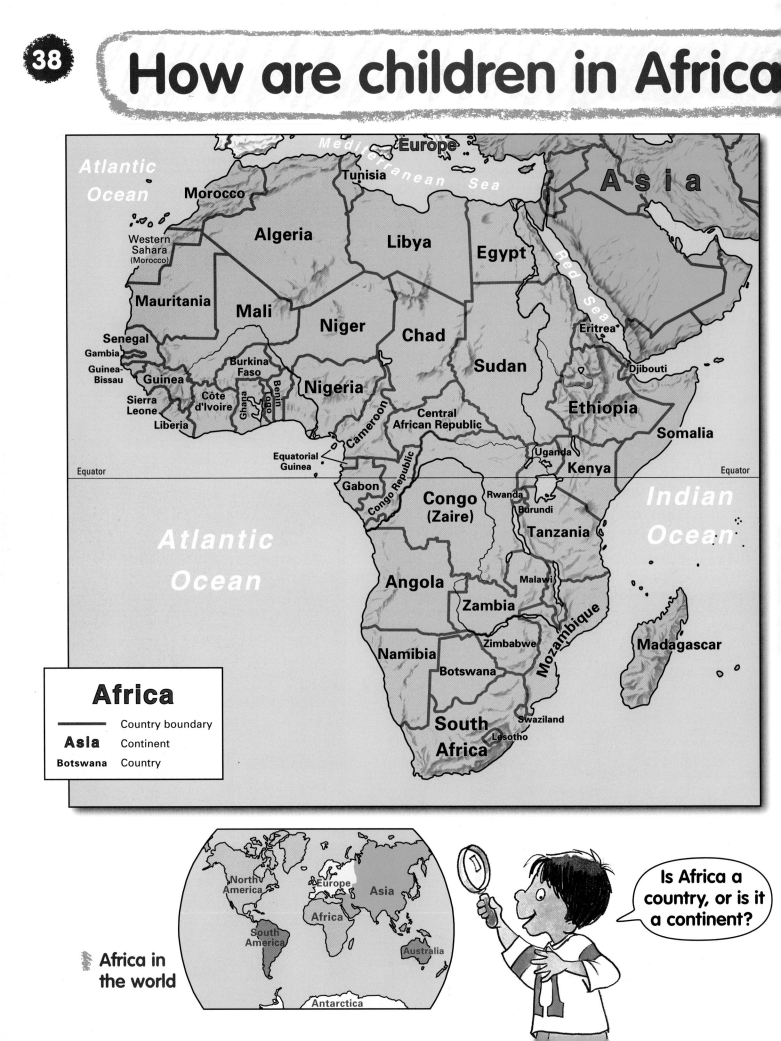

Africa

— Country boundary

Asia Continent

Botswana Country

Africa in the world

Is Africa a country, or is it a continent?

 like you?

39

Girl in Burkina Faso

Father and daughter in Egypt

Children in Mozambique

Boy in Morocco

Students in Kenya

How is YOUR classroom like this one?

How are children in

🎋 Girl in Germany

🎋 Girl in Greece

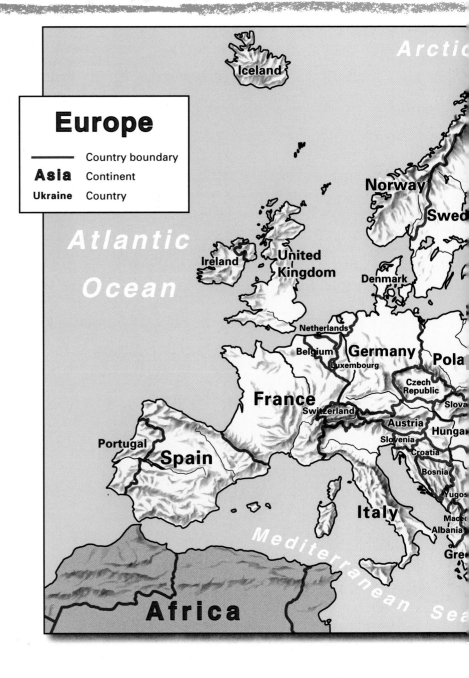

Europe

——— Country boundary
Asia Continent
Ukraine Country

Arctic

Iceland

Atlantic
Ocean

Norway

Swed

Ireland

United
Kingdom

Denmark

Pola

Netherlands

Belgium **Germany** Pola

Luxembourg

Czech
Republic

Slova

France

Switzerland

Austria Hunga

Slovenia

Portugal

Croatia

Spain

Bosnia

Yugos

Italy

Mace

Albania

Mediterranean Sea

Gre

Africa

Which continents
are neighbors
of Europe?

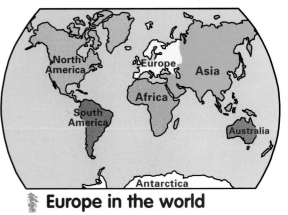

🎋 Europe in the world

Europe like you?

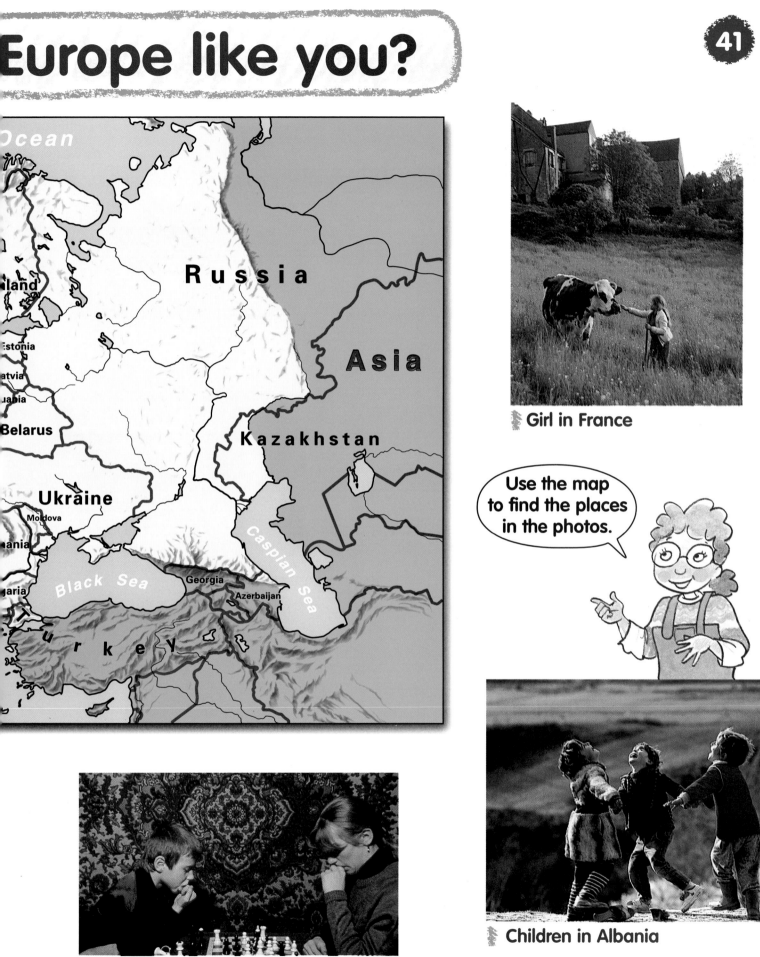

Girl in France

Use the map to find the places in the photos.

Mother and son in Russia

Children in Albania

How are children in Asia

Girl in the Philippines

What is YOUR favorite meal?

Family in Japan

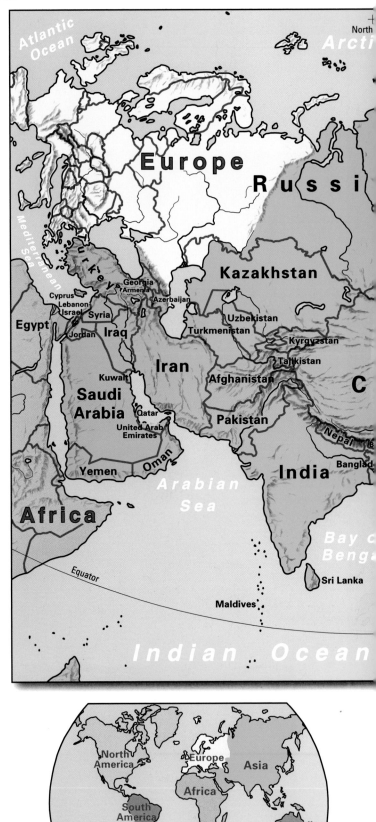

Asia in the world

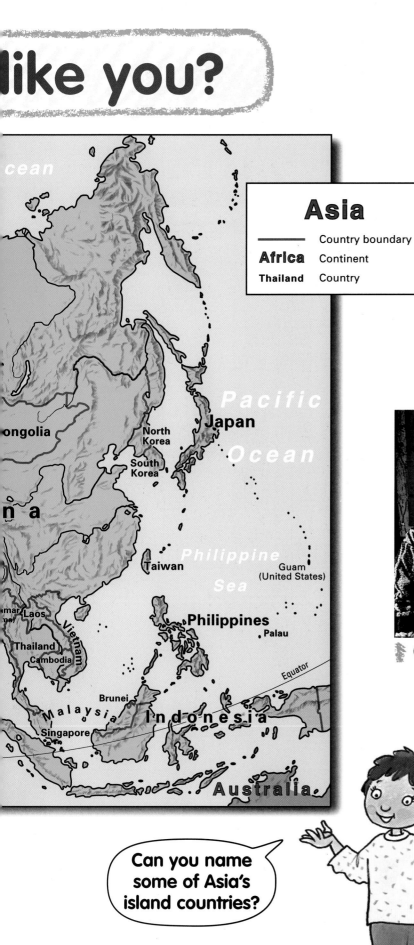

Asia

———	Country boundary
Africa	Continent
Thailand	Country

Pacific

Ocean

Japan

North
Korea

South
Korea

Mongolia

n a

Philippine

Taiwan

Guam
(United States)

Sea

mar Laos
pei

Vietnam

Philippines

Palau

Thailand
Cambodia

Equator

Brunei

Malaysia

Singapore

Indonesia

Australia

🎋 **Boy in Jordan**

🎋 **Children in Mongolia**

Can you name
some of Asia's
island countries?

🎋 **Girl in India**

Children in class

Boy with a pet

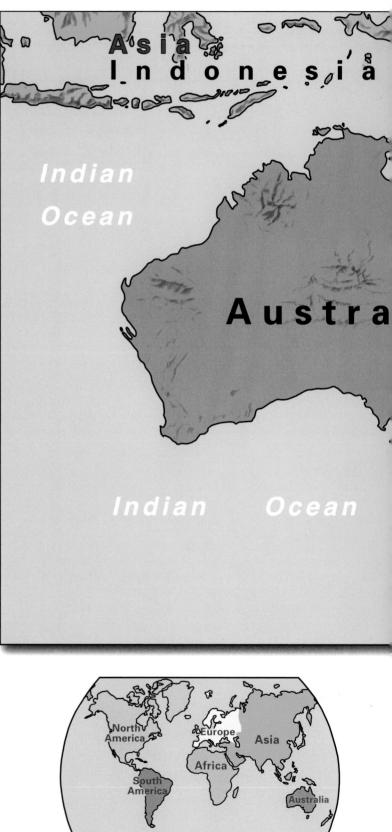
Asia
Indonesia

Indian
Ocean

Austra

Indian   Ocean

Do any other continents touch Australia?

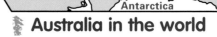
North America
Europe
Asia
Africa
South America
Australia
Antarctica

Australia in the world

Australia like you?

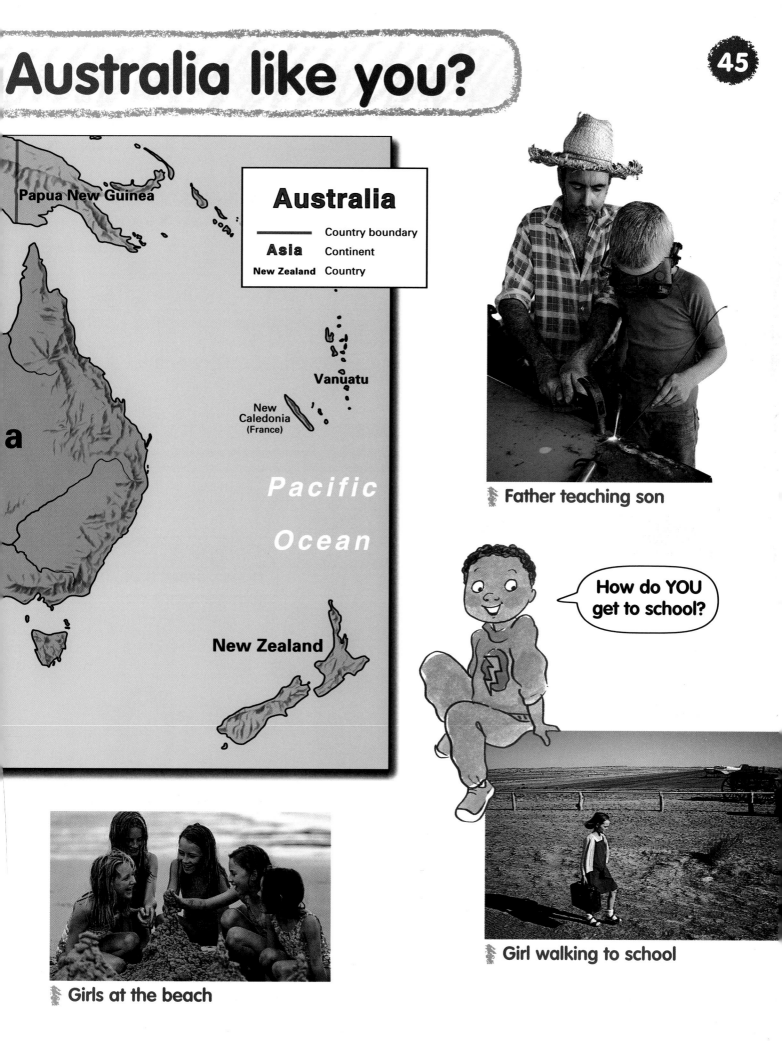

Australia

—— Country boundary

Asia Continent

New Zealand Country

Papua New Guinea

Vanuatu

New Caledonia (France)

Pacific Ocean

New Zealand

a

Father teaching son

How do YOU get to school?

Girls at the beach

Girl walking to school

Who lives in Antarctica?

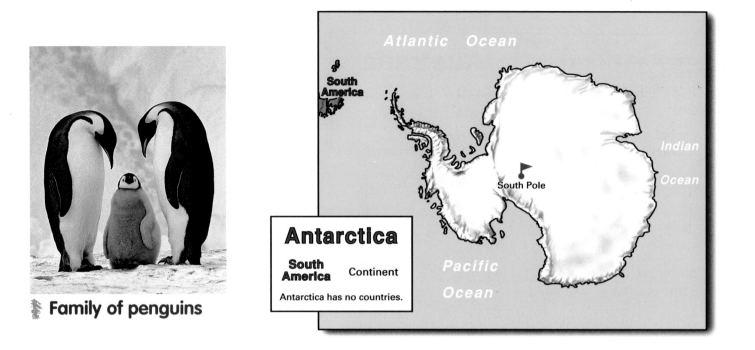

Family of penguins

Antarctica

South America · Continent

Antarctica has no countries.

Antarctica is covered with ice.

People do not have homes here, but penguins do!

Antarctica in the world

Glossary

A glossary tells what words mean.

atlas A book of maps.

boundary Where two states or countries meet.

capital City where the government of a country or state is located.

coastline The edge of a continent along a sea or an ocean.

continent One of the seven largest land areas on the earth. (See small map on page 46.)

country A land with one government. Some countries have many states.

Equator Imaginary line around the middle of the earth.

globe A model of the earth that is round like a ball.

lake A body of water, usually fresh. The water in a lake stays in one place.

map A special drawing of all or part of the earth as seen from above.

model A copy of an object, often smaller than the real thing.

mountain Part of the earth that is much taller than the land around it.

needs Things that make it possible to live.

neighborhood An area where people live.

ocean One of the four large bodies of salt water that cover most of the earth.

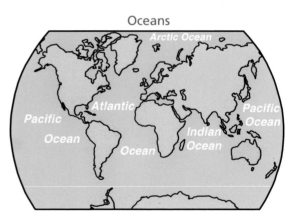

Oceans

Arctic Ocean

Atlantic

Pacific Ocean

Pacific Ocean

Indian Ocean

Ocean

river A long, narrow body of water. The water in a river flows downhill.

state Part of a country. There are 50 states in the United States of America.

wants Things that make life more fun.

All these words are used in the atlas.

Find countries here!

Index